The
CHARACTER
of
GOD

In His Own Words

JONATHAN G. EAST

WESTBOW
PRESS®
A DIVISION OF THOMAS NELSON
& ZONDERVAN

WestBow Press books may be ordered through booksellers or by contacting:

WestBow Press
A Division of Thomas Nelson & Zondervan
1663 Liberty Drive
Bloomington, IN 47403
www.westbowpress.com
1 (866) 928-1240

ISBN: 978-1-9736-3066-1 (sc)
ISBN: 978-1-9736-3067-8 (e)

Library of Congress Control Number: 2018906932

Print information available on the last page.

WestBow Press rev. date: 6/18/2018

Contents

Introduction

This work explores the character of God as revealed to Moses in Exodus, chapter 34, and will help His followers gain a better understanding of His attributes. The earthly ministry and works of Jesus Christ are also examined for comparison. I intend to show that Jesus always manifested the same characteristics His heavenly Father manifested. The implications I discuss will become obvious to those who are trying to live godly lives.

A proper understanding of the character, or heart, of God is of vital importance because it gives His followers a reference point for understanding all other things. A wrong understanding of God's character propagates a misunderstanding of all events of this world as well as all the plans God has for us in the world to come. It is only by knowing God's true character and experiencing personal fellowship with Him that we can put into proper perspective the events of this life and the eternal life to come.

A proper understanding of God's character, or nature, should cause His disciples to have proper reverence for Him. It should inspire them to always worship Him in spirit and in truth in all circumstances. God's children should look like Him. A proper understanding of His character should help His children conform to the image of His Son, Jesus, who was the earthly, visible image of the invisible God (Colossians 1:15).

Properly understanding God's personality should help His children become vessels of honor from which godly character should flow (2 Timothy 2:21).

There are many ideas today about God's character. The opinions vary widely. Some believe God created humanity but then sent us out alone with little concern for or any involvement in people's lives. But a detached and apathetic God is not the one true God described in the Holy Bible.

Others believe God predestined, or predetermined, all the events of the world and is domineering or strong-arming them into being. Those who follow this fatalistic view believe that humans have no choice in the events of their lives. But, of course, this is not the proper mind-set either. The God of the Holy Bible allows individuals to make choices that control their eternal destinies and bring much of the joy—or heartache—into life on this earth.

Even Christians totally devoted to God sometimes struggle to see the heart of God in proper perspective. This is especially true when facing suffering, loss, grief, persecution, and devastating tragedy.

Some people going through great tragedies are susceptible to the philosophy of Epicurus. Epicurus was a philosopher who lived between 341 and 270 BC. He posed the riddle, "Is God willing to prevent evil, but not able? Then he is impotent. Is he able, but not willing? Then he is malevolent. Is he both able and willing? Whence then is evil?"[1]

It is a sad reality and a monumental challenge that the followers of Jesus Christ must dispel heretical beliefs about the true and

---

[1] http://www.philosophyofreligion.com.

living God. If the Holy Bible is God's Word, and in it He meant to unveil Himself to His people, we must conclude there is a clear and somewhat complete description of Him within it. Although we may never come to a full understanding of God while we are living in the flesh, we must strive to know Him better and fellowship with Him more so that we can conform to His image and win the souls of those whose lives we touch.

It is not my intent to become deceived into believing that we can totally define God or to put Him in a box. But it is my earnest desire to expound on God's description of Himself and shed light on those aspects of His character.

To become knowledgeable about someone's character or personality, we could study the individual's history, methods, and ways. We might even ask his or her friends and associates about the person. We could learn from many sources. But the subject of interest knows himself or herself better than anyone else. Information gained from the original or primary source is usually judged to be the most accurate and credible. This is the source that is considered the most authoritative. The primary source has the most direct knowledge of the characteristics being described or investigated. We should always first look for data in primary sources.

Chapter 34 of the book of Exodus gives us God's firsthand account of Himself. This self-disclosure to Moses was not folklore or secondhand information. It was the God of the universe revealing direct knowledge about His character.

During Moses's earthly walk, he had an intense desire to know God deeply, not to merely know about Him. Moses was a humble man despite having been reared in the pharaoh's palace. And he was a man of deep faith in God (Hebrews 11:24–28). When God spoke to Moses from the burning bush, Moses reverenced the name of God (Exodus 3:6). Moses felt inadequate for the tasks ahead and humbly questioned and even protested with God about His new assignment. Moses probed to find out more about the God who came down to deliver the children of Israel from the oppressive hands of the

Egyptians and wished to use him as a tool for accomplishing this purpose. He wanted to better understand who God was and better convey this to the children of Israel.

> And Moses said unto God, Behold, when I come unto the children of Israel, and shall say unto them, The God of your fathers hath sent me unto you; and they shall say to me, What is his name? What shall I say unto them? And God said unto Moses, I am that I am: and he said, Thus shalt thou say unto the children of Israel, I am hath sent me unto you. (Exodus 3:13–14)

Moses began to know this self-existent God deeper and deeper as he led the children of Israel out of Egypt.

Though Moses started out by reluctantly surrendering to God's call, he humbly and faithfully listened and obeyed Him. He continually and prayerfully interceded for the children of Israel (Exodus 32:11–13, 31–32; 34:9). Although Moses witnessed many miraculous works of God and came to know God deeply as a deliverer, provider, sustainer, and great defender, he wanted to see even more of the glory of God. God's glory descended when Moses went to the tabernacle to seek the Lord (Exodus 33:9–11), but even this was not enough for Moses. Moses prayed for God's presence (Exodus 33:12–16) and to see the glory of God (Exodus 33:18).

God subsequently explained to Moses that no one could look at the face and full glory of God and live. But God graciously favored Moses's request with a plan. Moses would be allowed to stand upon a rock shielded by the hand of God, listen to God's powerful self-disclosure, and then see the back parts of God (Exodus 33:19–23).

How wonderful and gracious of God to honor Moses's request to know Him better! How great is His character, one who would protect Moses's weakness while revealing His strength! How gentle and gracious to reveal more of His infinite greatness to a finite mind!

I am in awe to know that God, in His infinite wisdom and goodness, gave a glimpse of His character and an explanation of His ways.

The thirty-fourth chapter of Exodus tells of the fulfillment of God's promised plan to Moses. Moses prepared himself, according to God's instructions, and went up Mount Sinai to meet with Him at the appointed time.

> And the LORD descended in the cloud, and stood with him there, and proclaimed the name of the LORD. And the LORD passed before him, and proclaimed The LORD, The LORD God, merciful and gracious, long-suffering, and abundant in goodness and truth, keeping mercy for thousands, forgiving iniquity and transgression and sin, and that will by no means clear the guilty; visiting the iniquity of the fathers upon the children, unto the third and to the fourth generation. (Exodus 34:6–7)

This passage of scripture is what I believe best explains the true nature, or character, of God. Let us now begin to dissect each statement of God in order to gain a better understanding, appreciation, and reverence for who He is. Let us look for the same attributes in Jesus. And let us see why this information is relevant to modern-day Christians.

The Lord

יְהוָה

As God descended in the cloud and stood with Moses at Mount Sinai, He proclaimed the name of the Lord (Exodus 34:5). Hebrew names have meaning; the name says something about the individual. There is strength in a proclamation. And there is much to be learned from the name of God.

The word *lord* appears in the Old Testament scriptures over six thousand times and in the New Testament over six hundred times. But a word of caution is in order. One must carefully check whether there is an uppercase or lowercase spelling when reading the Holy Bible. (There are many gods, but there is only one true and living God.) When written in all lowercase letters, the word *lord* generally refers to a human master or ruler. When written with a capitalized first letter, it is often translated to *Adonai*, which is God in His relationship to the earth. *Adonai* is the plural of *Adon*, meaning Lord, but does not refer to the proper name of God. When the word *lord* is written in scripture passages in all capital letters, such as in God's account of Himself in Exodus 34:6, it is the proper name of God. According to the website Hebrew for Christians, *Lord*, or the

Hebrew word *YHVH* (written by Moses before the use of vowels or vowel marks and later written as *YEHOVAH*) is the personal name of God, and His most frequent designation.

This proper name of God was so revered by the Hebrews that they avoided using it. They would often make a substitute for YHVH by using another title for God such as El-ohim or Adonai. When Hebrew scribes transcribed the ancient scrolls, they took special precautions before even writing the name YHVH. They stopped the writing process and went through a ceremonial cleansing process before writing the name.

The word *YHVH*, or *YEHOVAH*, was later changed to Yehovah, in order to make the pronunciation of it easier. This name Yehovah means "the eternal one." He is the immutable or unchangeable one. He is the God who was and is and is to come. He is the self-existent God. When God revealed Himself to Moses as Yehovah, He was saying all of that.

To be eternal is to be without beginning or end. God has always existed. He will always continue to be in existence. In Genesis 1:1, we see that God existed before the beginning of this temporal and material world: "In the beginning God created the heaven and the earth." Colossians 1:16 explains further that Jesus pre-existed His incarnation and was active in the creation: "For by him were all things created, that are in heaven, and that are in earth, visible and invisible, whether they be thrones, or dominions, or principalities, or powers; all things were created by him, and for him." Furthermore, the apostle Peter explained that the Son of God, Jesus, the creator of all things, was foreordained to be our redeemer, the spotless lamb of God, before the foundation of the world (1 Peter 1:18–20). The prophet Isaiah also spoke of God's eternal existence: "For thus saith the high and lofty One that inhabiteth eternity, whose name is Holy" (Isaiah 57:15).

Not only is God eternal, He is immutable. To be immutable is to be without change. James 1:17 states, "Every good gift and every perfect gift is from above, and cometh down from the Father of lights, with whom is no variableness, neither shadow of turning." There is absolutely no vacillation from one side to the other with the one true God. Time, situations, and circumstances do not alter the character of God. He is unshakable and immutable. Malachi 3:6 explains, "For I am the LORD, I change not." The writer of Hebrews also states, "Jesus Christ the same yesterday, and today, and for ever" (Hebrews 13:7).

It is altogether fitting and proper that the first thing we desire to know about another is the individual's name. It is my opinion that, each time God's proper name is used, there is an indication of His desire for a relationship with humankind. Throughout scripture, it has been God's desire for close fellowship with all humans. We were created for fellowship with God. In the garden of Eden, God came and walked with humans. When God gave instructions for the tabernacle, it was for the purpose of dwelling among His people: "And let them make me a sanctuary, that I may dwell among them" (Exodus 25:8). Even after this earth passes away, God wants to dwell with humanity:

> And I saw a new heaven and a new earth: for the first heaven and the first earth were passed away; and there was no more sea. And I, John, saw the holy city, new Jerusalem, coming down from God out of heaven, prepared as a bride adorned for her husband. And I heard a great voice out of heaven saying, Behold, the tabernacle of God is with men, and he will dwell with them, and they shall be his people, and God himself shall be with them, and be their God. (Revelation 21:1–3)

The use of God's proper name indicates the way He wishes to relate to humanity. His proper name is used in combination with ten other words in the Old Testament. When used this way, those other aspects of His character—or ways in which He blesses humankind—are highlighted. When God revealed Himself as Yehovah Yireh, He was saying that He is the eternal, unchangeable God who provides (Genesis 22:14). When He revealed Himself as Yehovah Ropheka in Exodus 15:26, He was saying that He is the eternal, unchangeable God who heals. His name is given as Yehovah Nissi in Exodus 17:15, meaning God, my eternal, unchangeable banner. Many times, God reveals Himself as Yehovah MeKaddishkem, the eternal, unchangeable God who sanctifies us (Exodus 31:13; Leviticus 20:8, 21:8, 22:32; Ezekiel 20:12). It is given as Yehovah Shalom in Judges 6:24, meaning the eternal, unchangeable God who sends peace. God is revealed to us as Yehovah ZeBa'oth, the eternal, unchangeable LORD of hosts (1 Samuel 1:3). We know that God is infinitely good and holy as He reveals Himself as Yehovah Zidenu, the eternal, unchangeable God of righteousness in Jeremiah 23:6 and 33:16. We come to know more about God's omnipresence and eternal existence when we see Him revealed as Yehovah Shammah, the God who is there (Ezekiel 48:35).We see Him revealed to us as God, the most high, or Yehovah 'Elyon, in Psalms 7:17, 47:2, and 97:9. And He revealed Himself to us as Yehovah Ro'I, the eternal, unchangeable God who is our shepherd in the well-known twenty-third Psalm.

Just a study of His name should bring disciples to praise His holy name! We have such tremendous reasons to be glad! I am so thankful to serve a God who is always there, seeing all of my circumstances. He is one who provides, protects, goes before me as a banner, and sends me peace. Let us always give credit to whom it is due! Our God should be praised for every good gift we enjoy (James 1:17).

The LORD God

יְהֹוָה אֵל

After introducing Himself to Moses by giving His proper name, God revealed His position as God, the LORD God. The original Hebrew word *El* means "the almighty." By being the almighty God, He separates Himself from any other. There is none like Him. Deuteronomy 6:4 declares, "Hear O Israel: The LORD our God is one LORD." There may be many gods of this world, but only the one who is almighty. Likewise, Isaiah 46:9 declares, "Remember the former things of old: for I am God, and there is none else; I am God, and there is none like me."

To be almighty is to have absolute power and omnipotence. There is nothing too difficult for the almighty God. Prophets of old have asked questions about God's almighty power, and God has answered with consistent affirmation concerning His omnipotence. Even God asks, as recorded in Jeremiah 32:27, "Behold, I am the LORD, the God of all flesh: is there any thing too hard for me?" He proceeds in the same passage to explain the imminent judgment on the city because of the inhabitants' evil doings and disobedience to the laws of God. Isaiah confirms the same omnipotence: "Behold, the Lord's hand is not shortened, that it cannot save, neither his ear heavy, that it cannot hear" (Isaiah 59:1). Isaiah 50:2 asks:

> Wherefore, when I came was there no man? When I called, was there none to answer? Is my hand shortened at all, that it cannot redeem? Or have I no power to deliver? Behold, at my rebuke I dry up the sea, I make the rivers a wilderness.

God is not just a little above every other. He is abundantly above every other. His ways and thoughts are higher than all others (Isaiah 55:9). And He is able to do exceeding abundantly above all that we ask or think (Ephesians 3:20).

The omnipotence of God is vastly underestimated and misunderstood. Many believe there has been an eternal struggle between good and evil, or God and Satan, since days of old. Some believe God is now getting ready or building up for the day ahead when He will ultimately defeat Satan. This mind-set does not accurately account for the greatness of God. For now, the Holy Spirit restrains, and God waits for the fullness of time.

At the God-appointed time, the world will witness no grand struggle between God and Satan. Satan is not a threat in power to the almighty God. Consider the simplicity of the beginning of the millennial reign as described in Revelation 20:1–3:

> And I saw an angel come down from Heaven, having the keys of the bottomless pit and a great chain in his hand. And he laid hold on the dragon, that old serpent, which is the Devil, and Satan, and bound him a thousand years. And cast him into the bottomless pit, and shut him up, and set a seal upon him, that he should deceive the nations no more, till the thousand years should be fulfilled: and after that he must be loosed a little season.

At the God-appointed time, Satan will be utterly consumed with the spirit of God's coming (2 Thessalonians 2:7–8). And at the God-appointed time, the great deceiver will deceive the nations no more. Satan's final destiny is revealed in Revelation 20:10: "And the devil that deceived them was cast into the Lake of fire and brimstone, where the beast and the false prophet are, and shall be tormented day and night for ever and ever."

God wanted Moses to know His proper name, His position, and His character. All these reveal His glory and help us to understand who He is. This is of utmost importance and relevance for Christians today.

We must always remember that God is still eternal and omnipresent. He is in existence and abiding with us today. We must never fear abandonment in a world where evil is ever present. God's very nature demands that He is still here and will always be. Just as surely as God kept His promises to Moses (Deuteronomy 31:3–6) and to Joshua (Joshua 1:5), He will keep His promises to us.

The New Testament writer of Hebrews reassures us, "Let your conversation be without covetousness; and be content with such things as ye have: for he hath said, I will never leave thee, nor forsake thee" (Hebrews 13:5). Our great commission includes the promise, straight from the mouth of our risen redeemer and Savior, Jesus Christ:

> Go ye therefore, and teach all nations, baptizing them in the name of the Father, and of the Son, and of the Holy Ghost: Teaching them to observe whatsoever I have commanded you: and, lo, I am with you alway, even unto the end of the world. Amen. (Matthew 28:19–20)

We must always be mindful that God is still immutable. He will never change. We can depend on His character, regardless of changing times, attitudes, and modern-day events. If it was God's character to want a relationship with Moses and to reveal Himself to Moses, then we can trust that He wants us to know Him also. The love that God had for Adam before the fall still endured after the fall. The love God had for Moses and the children of Israel during the wilderness journey endured in the Promised Land. God still loves humankind today. Though our sin necessitates that He deals with us each differently at times, His love endures. The apostle Paul explained God's enduring love this way to the Romans:

> Nay, in all things we are more than conquerors through him that loved us. For I am persuaded that neither death, nor life, nor angels, nor principalities, nor powers, nor things present, nor things to come, Nor height, nor depth, nor any other creature, shall be able to separate us from the love of God, which is in Christ Jesus our Lord. (Romans 8:37–39)

And Christians must always remember that we can depend on God's omnipotence. If He is eternal and unchangeable, He is most assuredly still almighty. Because of His almighty power, He can enable and help all people to do and accomplish what He calls them to do. We can do all things through Christ who strengthens us (Philippians 4:13).

We must remember that our weakness does not diminish His greatness. Indeed, His strength alone is glorified in our weakness. "And he said unto me, My grace is sufficient for thee: for my strength is made perfect in weakness. Most gladly therefore will I rather glory in my infirmities, that the power of Christ may rest upon me" (2 Corinthians 12:9). The same God who protected Shadrach, Meshach, and Abednego in the fiery furnace is still our God today, and He is still able to deliver us (Daniel 3).

Our omnipotent God is able to help us overcome the great gulf between a sinful person and a holy God. God has enabled us to have fellowship with Him, because of His glorious implemented plan. A plan for reconciliation was established before the foundation of the world was laid (1 Peter 1:20). We are blessed to be adopted by Jesus Christ according to the good pleasure of His will, and we have redemption from our sinful state through His blood. This forgiveness of our sins comes when we are convicted of our sinfulness by the sweet Holy Spirit, acknowledge and confess our sins to God, and have faith in His death as our substitution. This forgiveness because of His bloodshed is completely unmerited and exists only because of the riches of His grace (Ephesians 1:5–7). Paul further explains, "For by grace are ye saved through faith; and that not of yourselves: it is the gift of God, Not of works, lest any man should boast" (Ephesians 2:8–9). We are so blessed to be reconciled to a God who is eternal, immutable, and almighty.

The first two descriptions that God revealed to Moses apply only to God and are not to be imitated by humankind. No matter how godly people try to live, they will never be or become eternal, immutable, or almighty. These are God's qualities alone and should be worshipped.

But the next attributes God revealed are qualities for which Christians should strive. Christians were first called Christians at Antioch (Acts 11:26). This reference meant that they modeled Christlike behavior. Christians are supposed to conform to the image of Jesus Christ (Romans 8:29). The question then becomes, what did Christ look like? According to the words of Jesus, "If you have seen me, you have seen the Father" (John 14:9). The writer of Colossians also records, "In whom we have redemption through his blood, even the forgiveness of sins: Who is the image of the invisible God, the firstborn of every creature" (Colossians 1:14–15). Jesus was Immanuel, God incarnate who dwelled among us. He was the visible image of the invisible God. Jesus has always been of the same character as His Father, and we are to have the same character as Jesus.

Merciful

רַחוּם

After revealing His name and His position, God began to reveal to Moses His character and how He relates to humankind. What a calming truth was the proclamation that God is merciful! How it must have alleviated Moses's fears, and what a comfort he must have felt to hear a holy God say that He is merciful to sinful people! Moses knew of the fallen state of humankind, and he knew of the holiness of God (Exodus 3:2–6). Moses knew there was a price to be paid for sin. But, relieved to hear God speak of His mercy, Moses came to realize that the price would not have to be paid at that moment.

Mercy means that a holy God withholds from humankind that which humans rightly deserve. When dealing with the holiness of God, we don't need to be reminded of our sinfulness. It is ever apparent. When the glory and holiness of God is present, all people will feel like Isaiah: "Then said I, Woe is me! For I am undone, because I am a man of unclean lips, and I dwell in the midst of a people of unclean lips: for mine eyes have seen the King, the LORD of hosts" (Isaiah 6:5).

The original Hebrew word, here translated as "merciful," is

rachum (pronounced rakh-oom). According to the Bible study website studylight.org, it is also defined as love—to love deeply, to be compassionate, or to have tender affection. The idea being conveyed by this word is that of lovingly withholding judgment. When we stand guilty before God, we will not wish for justice but rather for mercy.

Because God is immutable, He has always been merciful and compassionate. This was the way He dealt with the fall of Adam (Genesis 3:9–21). This was the way God dealt with the children of Israel on numerous occasions. It has been His way of dealing with humankind all through the ages. And it is His mercy and compassion that stays His judgment on sinful people to this very day. Psalm 78:38 explains, "But he, being full of compassion, forgave their iniquity." The writer of Psalm 86:15 agrees: "But thou, O Lord, art a God full of compassion." The psalmist of Psalm 103 also declares, in verse 8, "The LORD is merciful and gracious, slow to anger, and plenteous in mercy." We should join the psalmists in praise for all the LORD's past and present blessings, especially because His mercy endures forever (Psalm 136).

It is very interesting to note that one of the first ways God related to humankind was with mercy. Indeed, if God would not withhold His judgment, there would certainly be no need for any of His other attributes or characteristics. God's mercy gives meaning to and purpose for His grace, longsuffering, goodness, and truth. Mercy is the conduit, so to speak, which allows all the other characteristics to flow from a holy God to sinful humankind. Without God's mercy, humankind could never live to enjoy all the rest of God's goodness.

Since Jesus is fully God, and He displays the same character as God the Father, then, of course, Jesus is merciful and compassionate. In fact, this is the way we see Jesus in all the Gospels, the historical books of Jesus's life on earth. Jesus always conducted Himself with mercy and compassion. When He saw the multitude as sheep having no shepherd, He was moved with compassion (Matthew 9:36; Mark 6:34). When He saw the sick and diseased, He was moved with compassion (Matthew 14:14; Mark 1:41). When Jesus witnessed the funeral procession of the widow of Nain's son, He was moved with compassion (Luke 7:11–16). I believe that even the expulsion of the money changers from the temple was motivated by righteous indignation and compassion for the poor people being overcharged and cheated (John 2:13–17). Although the pilgrims coming to Jerusalem to worship brought their own currencies, they did not bring animals to sacrifice. It is powerful and moving to remember that Jesus's earthly mother, Mary, and stepfather, Joseph, could afford only the poor people's sacrifice—two turtle doves (Luke 2:24). The scriptures are consistent and without error in recording Jesus's actions always being consistent with His Father's character. John records, "And there are also many other things which Jesus did, the which, if they should be written every one, I suppose that even the world itself could not contain the books that should be written. Amen" (John 21:25).

Mercy should flow freely from a Christian. Mercy has graciously been given to us. And although it was free to us, it cost a great price. It cost the life of God's only Son. As we have freely received, we should freely give. To have the character of God is to extend mercy to others. Jesus instructed in Luke 6:36, "Be ye therefore merciful, as your Father also is merciful." Allowing our own wrath or personal desires to dominate our lives is not consistent with conforming to Christ's model of behavior. Christians are not to be controlled by the flesh but by the Holy Spirit. They are not to be controlled by their own wills but to be obedient to the perfect will of God. James admonishes us, "Wherefore, my beloved brethren, let every man be swift to hear, slow to speak, slow to wrath: For the wrath of man worketh not the righteousness of God" (James 1:19–20).

Jesus affected the world in a marvelous way, and He did so by first extending mercy and having compassion on others. If Christians want to affect the world, especially those with whom they have daily contact, they first need to be merciful and compassionate. Each Christian would do well to be mindful of Romans 6:23: "For the wages of sin is death; but the gift of God is eternal life through Jesus Christ our Lord." We must remember that it is the mercy of God toward each of us that stays God's wrath from being poured out on our sinful lives. Jude instructs us to use compassion to make a difference in the lives of others: "Keep yourselves in the love of God, looking for the mercy of our Lord Jesus Christ unto eternal life. And of some have compassion, making a difference. And others save with fear, pulling them out of the fire; hating even the garment spotted by the flesh" (Jude 22).

If we have the proper compassion toward those who do not know the Lord, and if we do not ignore the urgency in the former phrases "pulling them out of the fire" (Jude 1:23) and "them that are drawn unto death, and those that are ready to be slain" (Proverbs 24:11), then we will extend loving mercy.

Moses certainly understood the desperate condition of the children of Israel, and he learned to be merciful during his walk with God. When God threatened to destroy them, Moses interceded by pleading for mercy toward them (Exodus 32:9–14). Modern-day Christians would do well to follow Moses's example of intercessory prayer.

Gracious

וְחַנּוּן

After revealing to Moses that He was merciful, God also was gracious. I define mercy as withholding from someone the punishment that is rightly deserved. Grace is kindness displayed by pouring out blessings that are not deserved or merited. Put very simply, it is unearned favor.

Moses must have stood trembling in the presence of the almighty God. He was certainly relieved to learn that God was merciful and thrilled to discover that He was also gracious! I am of the belief that God's self-disclosure or revelation to Moses was, in itself, an act of grace. God wants us to approach Him and to know Him.

Moses was a very learned man. He was intelligent and had been schooled by the finest educators in the pharaoh's palace. He had many privileges that were afforded only to those who dwelled in the home of the ruler. He probably had much time for studying and had many more luxuries in life than most of the children of Israel he led. Moses could certainly comprehend and record all the revelations from God.

Isn't it interesting that God Almighty, creator of the universe, would communicate in a way that could be understood by humankind? We know that for effective communication to occur, the language used in teaching must be common to the teacher and the learner.[2] God knows all things well, including our languages.

But we know that God is no respecter of persons (Acts 10:34). He doesn't favor a well-educated person over a lowly shepherd. Isn't it really magnificent that the hosts of heaven announced to the shepherds first the glorious news of Jesus's birth? We can rest assured that the very same God who created us and put us on a planet that He holds in orbit will know us intimately and be able to communicate with us effectively.

The original Hebrew word used here, translated as "gracious," is *channun* (pronounced kah-noon), which means "pleasantly kind, benevolent, and courteous." It is translated as "gracious" only in the Holy Bible. But according to studylight.org, it comes from the same stem word from which *favorable*, *fair*, and *pity* are derived. It is certainly a great gift from God that He would show favor, pity, loving kindness, and benevolence on sinful humankind, who are totally undeserving of all the favor.

Mercy is more than humankind could hope for. But grace is more than humankind could ever dream of! To receive anything other than judgment from a holy God is simply grace. It is no wonder that John Newton, who had once been a slave trader who dealt with the precious commodity of human beings with souls, would pair the word *grace* with *amazing*. As a struggling but sinful writer, I still find God's grace amazing!

God's pattern of dealing with sinful humankind has always been the same. He first displays His mercy and grace. It was God's infinite goodness that would devise a plan for redemption and reconciliation of humankind before He ever created them. It was grace that allowed

---

[2] John Milton Gregory, *The Seven Laws of Teaching* (1886), 52.

the promise of the Messiah in Genesis 3:15. And it is grace that allows each and every one who believes to partake of that gift. It is difficult for the finite mind to comprehend the depths of God's loving favor toward humankind. Yet, we know "for God so loved the world, that he gave his only begotten Son, that whosoever believeth in him should not perish, but have everlasting life" (John 3:16). We also believe that "for by grace are ye saved through faith, and that not of yourselves: it is the gift of God: Not of works, lest any man should boast" (Ephesians 2:8–9). It is the grace of God that brings salvation (Titus 2:11). It is the grace of God that He would accept the precious blood of His sinless, holy Son, Jesus, as the atonement for our sin.

At least eight different times in the Old Testament, God is described as being gracious and merciful. Psalm 116:5 records it: "Gracious in the LORD, and righteous, yea, our God is merciful." If way say that mercy is the conduit that allows all blessings to flow through to humankind, we must see His grace as the wire that transfers every single favor.

We always see Jesus bearing the same characteristic as His heavenly Father, especially in being gracious. Twelve times in the New Testament the phrase "the grace of our Lord Jesus" appears (Romans 16:20, 24; 1 Thessalonians 5:28; 2 Thessalonians 1:12, 3:18; 1 Timothy 1:14; Philemon 1:25; Revelation 22:21). Interestingly, it appears in the last verse of the Holy Bible: "The grace of our Lord Jesus Christ be with you all. Amen" (Revelation 22:21).

Jesus's incarnation was the very means of grace that John the Baptist spoke of in John 1:15–17: "This was he of whom I spake, He that cometh after me is preferred before me: for he was before me. And of his fullness have all we received, and grace for grace. For the law was given by Moses, but grace and truth came by Jesus Christ."

We see Jesus repeatedly giving unmerited favor and grace to His disciples. Though the apostles were committed, they struggled to understand Jesus's teachings and to be faithful and obedient to His commands. He patiently gave further explanations and sometimes loving rebukes (Matthew 16:23, 19:14; Luke 8:25, 9:55).

We see Jesus giving unmerited favor to the woman caught in the very act of adultery (John 3–11). We see Jesus giving grace to a different woman whose sins were many, and to the hypocritical, self-righteous Pharisee, Simon, who inwardly condemned her (Luke 7:36–50).

We know that Jesus's death was the ultimate gift of grace to all. For we know that we are all guilty of sin:

> For all have sinned, and come short of the glory of God; Being justified freely by his grace through the redemption that is in Christ Jesus: Whom God hath set forth to be a propitiation through faith in his blood, to declare righteousness for the remission of sins that are past, through the forbearance of God; To declare, I say, at this time his righteousness; that he might be just, and the justifier of him which believeth in Jesus. (Romans 3:23–26)

Grace is also expected of Christians. Jesus commanded that we show grace: "Love your enemies, do good to them which hate you, Bless them that curse you, and pray for them which despitefully use you" (Luke 6:27–28). Paul instructed the Corinthians to abound in grace (2 Corinthians 8:7–8). He instructed the Ephesians to minister grace (Ephesians 4:29). And he instructed the Colossians to speak with grace (Colossians 4:2–6). The apostle Peter also admonished us to "grow in grace, and in the knowledge of our Lord and Saviour Jesus Christ. To him be glory both now and for ever. Amen" (2 Peter 3:18).

Longsuffering

אֶרֶךְ

Thus far, we have discovered God's self-disclosure of His proper name, His position, and two of His many characteristics. Next, God revealed yet another loving response to humankind's sinful nature. If it weren't for our frailties and sinful behavior, there would be no need for God to be longsuffering. If we were always faithful, obedient, and holy, then we wouldn't require such patience. Praises be to God that He loves us in spite of how we are!

The Hebrew term translated here as "longsuffering" is *'erekh 'appayim* (pronounced ark-aphim). According to studylight.org, this term is interestingly translated five different ways in the Old Testament: "longsuffering," "slow to anger," "slow to wrath," "patient" (Ecclesiastes 7:8), and "long-winged" (Ezekiel 17:3). The ideas being expressed are to be slow in getting angry, to be patient, and to be able to endure aggravation for long periods of time. The Ezekiel reference to being long-winged is used to show how an eagle can sustain flight for long periods of time by using the air currents and not exerting its own energy.

When Moses comprehended God's revelation thus far, it may

have felt like this: "I am the eternal, unchangeable, and Almighty God. I will withhold my judgments. I will extend my blessings. And I will be tolerant of your faults and weakness." Because Moses had an awareness of his own sinful state, and that of the children of Israel, he must have been shouting with joy to hear about such an awesome God! We do know that he had the proper response of worship (Exodus 34:8). No wonder his face shone with the glory of God after this encounter!

If God were not willing to be merciful to us and extend His favor to us, then He would not need to be longsuffering. To serve the omnipotent God is a high calling. But to serve an eternal, unchanging, and almighty God who is merciful, gracious, and longsuffering toward us is an awesome privilege! It was for Moses, and it is for Christians today.

It is apparent throughout the Holy Bible that God is longsuffering toward humankind. Each time humankind has chosen to rebel rather than to obey, God's patience is required to deal with the rebellion and disobedience. The first man, Adam, proved God's longsuffering. Though God showed many miracles, powerful deliverances, and victories to the children of Israel, they murmured and complained continuously. When King David, a man after God's own heart, committed adultery and murder, God proved His longsuffering with him. When the apostle Peter denied any association with Jesus, God proved His longsuffering with him.

It is interesting and striking that Jonah actually expressed his frustration and displeasure with God regarding God's longsuffering toward the inhabitants of the large city of Nineveh. When the sinful inhabitants repented and God spared the city, Jonah had a lot to say about it:

> But it displeased Jonah exceedingly, and he was very angry. And he prayed unto the LORD, and said, I pray thee, O LORD, was not this my saying, when I was yet in my country? Therefore I fled before unto

Tarshish: for I knew that thou art a gracious God, and merciful, slow to anger, and of great kindness, and repentest thee of the evil. (Jonah 4:1–2)

God had to deal with Jonah's lack of pity toward the Ninevites. Perhaps Jonah's heart might have been right with God and his prayers might have been more God-honoring had he been reflective of his deliverance from the fish's belly. Each one of us should be very thankful for God's willingness to be longsuffering.

When speaking of Israel, the psalmist said:

For their heart was not right with him, neither were they stedfast in his covenant. But he, being full of compassion, forgave their iniquity, and destroyed them not: yea, many a time turned he his anger away, and did not stir up all his wrath. For he remembered that they were but flesh; a wind that passeth away, and cometh not again. (Psalm 78:37–39)

The apostle Peter described God's longsuffering this way: "The Lord is not slack concerning his promise, as some men count slackness; but is longsuffering to us-ward, not willing that any should perish, but that all should come to repentance" (2 Peter 3:9). Would that the Holy Spirit would allow this verse to leap into our minds each and every time we get a little Jonah-type attitude about the sinfulness of the individuals of the world in which we live. We might not have ended up in a great fish's belly, but most of us have sure gotten into some terrible conditions before we repented and cried out to God!

Jesus was always a great example of longsuffering toward others. His patience is most noticeable to me when I read about the way He dealt with His disciples. The ninth chapter of Luke tells of Jesus teaching the disciples about humility and service making us great. But just a few short verses later, we see them wanting to be powerful as they request that Jesus allow them to call fire down from heaven to consume people.

The sixteenth chapter of Matthew records the great confession of Peter to Jesus— "Thou art the Christ, the son of the living God" (Matthew 16:16)—and yet a few short verses later, we see Peter rebuking Jesus, and trying to tell Jesus how things are going to be! Jesus responded with a rebuke, but also with a longsuffering explanation about Peter's mistake. He explained that Peter had his mind on earthly things rather than things of God (Matthew 16:23). We would all do well to heed this rebuke from time to time.

Not only was Jesus longsuffering and tolerant toward His disciples but He was the same way toward the general public and the large crowds that followed and pressed in on Him everywhere He went. In the eighth chapter of Luke, we find the account of Jesus with Jairus, his gravely ill daughter, and the woman with the issue of blood who reached out and touched the hem of Jesus's garment. As Jairus was leading Jesus to his house so Jesus could heal his young daughter, the crowd pressed in on Him so much that the disciples thought it odd for Him to stop and check to see who had touched Him (Luke 8:41–48). Though the press of the crowd must have been hard to endure, Jesus was longsuffering toward the individuals within the crowd. The woman who had suffered from her bleeding problem for twelve years found healing in Jesus that day. Jesus was pleased with her faith and revealed to her that God rewards those who diligently seek Him (Hebrews 11:6).

The second chapter of Mark records the four friends carrying their friend to Jesus on a portable bed of sorts. The crowd pressed in so much that they couldn't get their friend close to Jesus. They took the drastic measure to carry him to the top of the house, tear the roof off, and lower their friend to Jesus! Jesus was longsuffering with the crowd and displayed His great grace and mercy to the man. He not only healed the man's body but forgave his sins. What a great God who pours out His blessings even more than we ask!

When the crowd came to arrest Jesus on the night of His betrayal,

He went in peace and longsuffering toward their wrongdoing, thus fulfilling His plan for our redemption. Jesus was always a perfect model of longsuffering.

Being longsuffering toward others is an attribute for which all Christians should strive. Galatians 5:22–23 states, "But the fruit of the Spirit is love, joy, peace, longsuffering, gentleness, goodness, faith, meekness, temperance: against such there is no law." Every good Christian should want to bear much fruit for God.

The apostle Paul instructed the Ephesians to deal with others humbly, gently, and with longsuffering, forbearing one another in love (Ephesians 4:2). Paul explained to the Colossians that longsuffering proved some spiritual maturity and fruitfulness:

> That ye might walk worthy of the Lord unto all pleasing, being fruitful in every good work, and increasing in the knowledge of God; Strengthened with all might, according to his glorious power, unto all patience and longsuffering with joyfulness. (Colossians 1:10–11)

Paul further admonished the Colossians to treat each other with longsuffering and forgiveness, reminding them that Christ had forgiven each of them:

> Put on therefore, as the elect of God, holy and beloved, bowels of mercies, kindness, longsuffering; Forbearing one another, and forgiving one another, if any man have a quarrel against any; even as Christ forgave you, so also do ye. (Colossians 3:12–13)

Christians should be longsuffering with the unsaved, realizing their natural state or condition, and remembering from whence we came. And Christians must strive to be longsuffering and patient toward our brothers and sisters in Christ. This is more difficult sometimes, as we expect more from Christian people. We must each try to remember that God is still daily being longsuffering toward us.

It is noteworthy that, while remaining longsuffering with sinners, Jesus never condoned, accepted, or minimized sin. Jesus never justified sinful behavior as being acceptable or all right. He is seen forgiving the repentant sinner. The Holy Bible does not command us to declare sin to be acceptable, or that each person be allowed to do what is right in his or her own eyes. But it does command us to be longsuffering with each other.

Abundant in Goodness

אַפַּיִם וְרַב־חֶסֶד

The first two revelations of God's character to Moses were somewhat to the point, straightforward, and matter of fact: I am God, the eternal one. I am the almighty God, omnipotent and immutable. The tone then seems to soften to me: I am also merciful, gracious, and longsuffering. Then, for me, the tone softens yet again, and would be quite comforting for a sinful man standing in the presence of a holy God. God proclaims to Moses that He is "abundant in goodness" (Exodus 34:6).

The original word used for "abundant" is the Hebrew word rab, meaning, "marked by great plenty."[3] According to studylight. org, in the Holy Bible, forms of this Hebrew word are translated to "great," "many," "much," "more," "long," "multitude," "greater," and "mighty." This word carries the idea of an amount that is beyond understanding. God's goodness is marked by great plenty. What an exciting revelation to know about someone who has absolute power!

---

[3] *Webster's Dictionary.*

Omnipotence in the wrong hands would be disastrous. But in the possession of a holy God, this knowledge gives incredible strength and hope to God's children.

Checed (pronounced kheh'·sed) is the Hebrew word used for "goodness." According to studylight.org, this word can be translated as "good," "goodness," "favor," "kindness," "kindly," "loving kindness," and "mercy." *Goodness* is a word best translated into action, such as a way of behaving or conducting affairs. How many times throughout the Holy Bible, could we most succinctly praise God for His marvelous works by simply saying that God is good!

The word *checed* is frequently used to describe the character of God. The prophet Micah asks, "Who is a God like unto thee, that pardoneth iniquity, and passeth by the transgression of the remnant of his heritage? He retaineth not his anger for ever, because he delighteth in mercy" (Micah 7:18). The last word, *mercy*, in the Hebrew version is *checed*. The book of Psalms uses this word more than 125 times. His paths are described as mercy in Psalm 25:10. His loving kindness is excellent in Psalm 36:10. Psalm 86:15 states that He is plenteous in mercy and truth. Psalm 107 is a great study of the goodness of God, as the word *checed* is used six times throughout. Four times it is used the same way: "Oh that men would praise the LORD for his goodness, and for his wonderful works to the children of men" (Psalm 107:8, 15, 21, 31). His goodness is proved by His works.

God's works are good because He is totally and completely good. That is His core character. The apostle John explains that there is no evil in Him at all. "This is the message which we have heard of him, and declare unto you, that God is light, and in him is no darkness at all" (1 John 1:5).

God is also described as good in the New Testament. Three of the four gospel writers (Matthew, Mark, and Luke) record Jesus's statement confirming that "there is none good but one, that is God" (Matthew 19:17; Mark 10:18; Luke 18:19). The goodness of God is well documented by the gospel writers, Matthew, Mark, Luke, and John, and in the book of the Acts of the Apostles. It is also proclaimed and explained by the letters to the early churches. James tells us of God's goodness and giving nature: "Every good gift and every perfect gift is from above, and cometh down from the Father of lights, with whom is no variableness, neither shadow of turning" (James 1:17).

Peter testified of Jesus's goodness and good works:

> That word, *I say*, ye know, which was published throughout all Judaea, and began from Galilee, after the baptism which John preached; How God anointed Jesus of Nazareth with the Holy Ghost and with power: who went about doing good, and healing all that were oppressed of the devil; for God was with him. (Acts 10:37–38)

The gospel writer Matthew tells us of Jesus's life after His baptism. As He traveled, He went about teaching, preaching, healing, and doing good works. Jesus went about with a determined purpose: "For the Son of man is come to seek and to save that which was lost" (Luke 19:10). Jesus conducted His life above reproach. He always displayed good works and never sinned. Because Jesus lived and walked among humankind, He has a unique compassion as our high priest. The writer of Hebrews tells us, "For we have not an high priest which cannot be touched with the feeling of our infirmities; but was in all points tempted like as we are, yet without sin" (Hebrews 4:15).

Jesus testified of God's goodness. "Many good works have I showed you from my Father" (John 10:32). "Believe me that I am in the Father, and the Father in me; or else believe me for the very works' sake" (John 14:11). Jesus did many good works because He was abundant in goodness.

As Christians striving to be like Christ, it is imperative that we strive to be filled with goodness and to do good works. Living in a sinful world makes it difficult to be filled with the right input. We need to be diligent about daily renewing our minds. Paul explained to the Romans, "And be not conformed to this world: but be ye transformed by the renewing of your mind, that ye may prove what is that good, and acceptable, and perfect, will of God" (Romans 12:2).

It is interesting that the golden rule was not given in the negative. Jesus did not simply say to avoid doing bad things to others; rather, He commanded in the positive: "And as ye would that men should do to you, do ye also to them likewise" (Luke 6:31). Matthew, chapter 5, gives some guidelines for Christian behavior. Jesus concludes by saying, "That ye may be the children of your Father which is in heaven" (Matthew 5:45). It is always a good father's desire that his children resemble him. This is no less true for God and His children.

The apostle Paul had much to say to the Galatians about Christians doing good work. He encouraged them not to grow weary or discouraged. "And let us not be weary in well doing; for in due season we shall reap, if we faint not" (Galatians 6:9).

When Christians do good works, it is only because of God's goodness in us. We, like the apostle Paul, know that there is no good in our own flesh. "For I know that in me Cthat is, in my flesh,) dwelleth no good thing: for to will is present with me; but how to perform that which is good I find not" (Romans 7:18). When good works are done, it is by God's strength and to His pleasure. And He alone should get the glory:

> Now the God of peace, that brought again from the dead our Lord Jesus, that great shepherd of the sheep, through the blood of the everlasting covenant, Make you perfect in every good work to do his will, working in you that which is wellpleasing in his sight, through Jesus Christ; to who be glory for ever and ever. Amen. (Hebrews 13:20–21)

The apostle Peter agreed and spoke of the good witness to others:

> Dearly beloved, I beseech you as strangers and pilgrims, abstain from fleshly lusts, which war against the soul; Having your conversation honest among the Gentiles: that, whereas they speak against you as evildoers, they may by your good works, which they shall behold, glorify God in the day of visitation. (1 Peter 2:11–12)

8

Abundant in Truth

אַפַּיִם וֶאֶמֶת:

Not only is God abundant in goodness but He is abundant in truth (Exodus 34:6). He is not only marked by a great plenty of truth but He is absolute truth. In addition to all the other things Moses learned about God's character, he soon learned that God is totally trustworthy because He is absolute truth. The Hebrew word translated as "truth" can also mean "firmness" and "faithfulness." With this solid character, it is no wonder that we refer to God as our rock: "For who is God, save the Lord? And who is a rock save our God?" (2 Samuel 22:32). The writer continues, "The Lord liveth; and blessed by my rock; and exalted be the God of the rock of my salvation" (2 Samuel 22:47).

Just as assuredly as there is no evil in God, we know there is no untruth in God. He is undefiled and holy. He is pure and full of perfect truth. Because of His absolute truth, we should ascribe greatness to Him, worship Him, and praise Him. "Because I will publish the name of the LORD: ascribe ye greatness unto our God. He is the Rock, his work is perfect: for all his ways are judgment: a God of truth and without iniquity, just and right is he" (Deuteronomy 32:3–4). Humankind can put complete trust in God's Word and never be let down.

Not only is God a God of absolute truth but He is a God that abhors untruth. The sixth chapter of Proverbs lists things God hates. Though *hate* is a strong word, it was the chosen word to be used in describing God's feelings about these things:

> These six things doth the LORD hate: yea, seven are an abomination unto him: A proud look, a lying tongue, and hands that shed innocent blood, An heart that deviseth wicked imaginations, feet that be swift in running to mischief, A false witness that speaketh lies, and he that soweth discord among brethren. (Proverbs 6:16–19)

It is noteworthy that untruth is referenced twice. Of the Ten Commandments written upon the stone tablets, God was purposeful to include a commandment to avoid being untruthful (Exodus 20:16).

Jesus's life on earth as Immanuel, God with us, was a perfect example of truth. As the visible image of God, He was abundant and absolute in truth. Jesus's every word was uttered in truth, and every deed carried out in truth. Truth was not just a concept that Jesus embraced. Truth was Jesus's character and being. It is who He is today. Jesus testified of this: "Jesus saith unto him, I am the way, the truth, and the life: no man cometh unto the Father, but by me" (John 14:6).

The holy scriptures make it undeniably clear and irrefutable that Jesus was the sinless and perfect sacrifice for the redemption of the souls of humankind. Jesus never broke any of the Mosaic laws or God's commandments. Jesus fulfilled the law (Matthew 5:17–18).

Jesus was tempted in all ways, as we are, "yet without sin" (Hebrews 4:15). He was without spot when He offered Himself as a sacrifice. "How much more shall the blood of Christ, who through the eternal Spirit offered himself without spot to God, purge your conscience from dead works to serve the living God?" (Hebrews 9:14). The apostle Peter agreed:

> For even hereunto were ye called: because Christ also suffered for us, leaving us an example, that ye should follow his steps: Who did no sin, neither was guile found in his mouth: Who, when he was reviled, reviled not again: when he suffered, he threatened not: but committed himself to him that judgeth righteously. (1 Peter 2:21–23)

The letters to the early churches gave strong charges to be truthful. They are part of our New Testament of Jesus Christ and are still strong charges to us today. The apostle Paul instructed the Colossians:

> But now ye also put off all these; anger, wrath, malice, blasphemy, filthy communication out of your mouth. Lie not one to another, seeing that ye have put off the old man with his deeds; And have put on the new man, which is renewed in knowledge after the image of him that created him. (Colossians 3:8–10)

The character of a Christian should be marked by a changed life. Though once a man lied, he should now tell the truth. Becoming a new creature in Christ will transform an individual so much that things look different than before. "Therefore if any man be in Christ, he is a new creature: old things are passed away; behold, all things are new" (2 Corinthians 5:17).

Since we have knowledge that God hates lies and lying, and since God has commanded us to be truthful, it should be every Christian's desire and intent to be honest and truthful in all matters.

We should want to be pleasing unto Him. Our greatest ally in keeping us honest is the Holy Spirit. The Holy Spirit is fully God and is called the Spirit of truth (John 14:17, 15:26, 16:13). The Holy Spirit abides within every true believer, and He leads each believer into all truth. Jesus explained:

> Howbeit when he, the Spirit of truth, is come, he will guide you into all truth: for he shall not speak of himself; but whatsoever he shall hear, that shall he speak: and he will shew you things to come. He shall glorify me: for he shall receive of mine, and shall shew it unto you. (John 16:13–14)

We must be vigilant to guard ourselves and others from untruth. The gospel of Jesus Christ is never advanced by untruth. When untruth is exposed, both the false messenger and the message lose credibility in the eyes of the witnesses.

We must insist that our worship of God is truthful. Truth is the way in which Jesus said the Father must be worshipped. "God is a spirit; and they that worship him must worship him in spirit and in truth" (John 4:24).

9

Keeping Mercy for Thousands

נֹצֵר חֶסֶד לָאֲלָפִים

God's self-disclosure broadens at this point to explain examples of His character in action. Moses knew who God was, His proper name and position, and some of His characteristics. Now God revealed more of His glorious character. In essence, God explained how His character was shown to humankind.

To me, God beautifully and graciously answered Moses's requests during this encounter. Let us recall Moses's pleas: "Now therefore, I pray thee, if I have found grace in thy sight, shew me now thy way, that I may know thee, that I may find grace in thy sight: and consider that this nation is thy people" (Exodus 33:13). "And he said, I beseech thee, shew me thy glory" (Exodus 33:18). In our finite minds, we sometimes believe that someone's glory lies in what we see or in some form of external beauty. But God's glory lies in who He is and how He is!

It is good to be mindful of the vast multitude of people that Moses was leading. According to Exodus 12:37, about six hundred thousand men came out on foot, and this does not account for the women and children. It is probable that over two million people came out of Egypt. Moses heard constant murmuring and complaining from them (Exodus 15, 16). He saw their idolatry (Exodus 32), and he witnessed much of the sinful behavior of the children of Israel. Though they had seen many miracles, they frequently lost sight of God and focused on their current situation. Moses had intervened on behalf of the Israelites when God had threatened to destroy them (Exodus 32:9–12). When God used the phrase "keeping mercy for thousands," (Exodus 34:7) it was a great reassurance to Moses that God's mercy and grace would be sufficient. If Moses had been concerned that God's mercy and loving kindness would not be adequate to cover this large number of habitually backsliding people, God assured him that His grace was sufficient.

Keeping mercy for thousands is a promise of God and a description of God's character. He promises that humankind will not exhaust the extent of His mercy. The mercy of God endures forever and to all generations (Psalm 136). God does not delight in the death of the wicked (Ezekiel 33:11). He is merciful, gracious, and longsuffering in trying to woo all unsaved people to repentance, belief, and salvation. His mercy extends to the vilest sinner, to those who have committed the most heinous sins. Nothing is too difficult for God. He is not willing that any should perish, but that all should come to repentance (2 Peter 3:9). God's mercy is absolutely sufficient and enduring.

Forgiving Iniquity, Transgression, and Sin

נֹשֵׂא עָוֹן וָפֶשַׁע וְחַטָּאָה

God's mercy is confirmed by His willingness to forgive. God proclaimed to Moses that He was willing to forgive iniquity, transgression, and sin (Exodus 34:7). Yet we know that sin cannot go unnoticed or unpunished by a holy and righteous God. It must be paid for. And the wages of sin is death (Romans 6:23).

Let us examine the forgiveness of God. According to studylight. org, to forgive means "to take away," "to bear up," or "to carry off." It does not mean to simply dismiss and forget. When sin is taken away from one, it must be placed on another. To forgive one of sin is to shift the penalty to another. Sinful humanity was blessed to have a volunteering substitute to take their place. Jesus was willing to bear the sins for the whole world. And He made this decision before He made humankind (1 Peter 1:20).

The true concept of forgiveness was taught to the children of Israel as God instructed Moses in the law. The Mosaic laws involved the sacrifice of perfect, spotless, and innocent little firstborn animals for the sins of the people. The writer of Hebrews explained that God took no pleasure in the blood of bulls and goats, and that it was not possible for their blood to take away sins (Hebrews 10:4–6). Paul explained it further to the Galatians, "Wherefore the law was our schoolmaster to bring us unto Christ, that we might be justified by faith" (Galatians 3:24). We see, then, the sacrifice of the little animals was a picture or symbol of what our real Savior would do. The blood of the animals didn't bring salvation. Faith that the true Messiah or Savior would come—that is what brought salvation. We are still saved by faith, now knowing that our Messiah did come.

The apostle Peter explained it further:

> Forasmuch as ye know that ye were not redeemed with corruptible things, as silver and gold, from your vain conversation received by tradition from your fathers; But with the precious blood of Christ, as a lamb without blemish and without spot. (1 Peter 1:18–19)

It is sad news that we all commit sin. But it is great news that we can be forgiven! Our sins can be forgiven because the penalty for our sin has already been paid! If we repent and confess our sins to God, we can be assured He will forgive us of our sins: "If we say that we have no sin, we deceive ourselves, and the truth is not in us. If we confess our sins, he is faithful and just to forgive us our sins, and to cleanse us from all unrighteousness" (1 John 1:8–9). The psalmist declares that God is ready to forgive: "For thou, Lord, art good, and ready to forgive; and plenteous in mercy unto all them that call upon thee" (Psalm 86:5). The prophet Isaiah explained that no sin is so bad that God will not welcome us: "Come now, and let us reason together, saith the LORD; though your sins be as scarlet, they shall be as white as snow; though they be red like crimson, they shall be as wool" (Isaiah 1:18).

God loves as a very good Father who is patiently waiting for His wayward children. The psalmist used this comparison:

> He hath not dealt with us after our sins; nor rewarded us according to our iniquities. For as the heaven is high above the earth, so great is his mercy toward them that fear him. As far as the east is from the west, so far hath he removed our transgressions from us. Like a father pitieth his children, so the LORD pitieth them that fear him. (Psalm 103:10–13)

Exodus 34:7 states that God will forgive iniquities, transgression, and sin. At first glance, this statement seems redundant. Why should sin be listed three times in one statement? Closer examination reveals these are varying stages of rebellion against God.

According to studylight.org, iniquity implies that there is very strong bondage involved in this degree of sin. It implies there is depravity, perversion, and outright rebellion toward God. When King David wrote Psalm 31, he cried out to God in agony over his iniquities:

> Have mercy upon me, O LORD, for I am in trouble: mine eye is consumed with grief, yea, my soul and my belly. For my life is spent with grief, and my years with sighing: my strength faileth because of mine iniquity, and my bones are consumed. (Psalm 31:9–10)

He relates in Psalm 38 that his iniquities are too much to bear: "For mine iniquities are gone over mine head: as a heavy burden they are too heavy for me" (Psalm 38:4). David gives the impression that his iniquities have taken him into bondage, and he has become helpless in the matter: "For innumerable evils have compassed me about: mine iniquities have taken hold upon me, so that I am not able to look up; they are more than the hairs of mine head; therefore my heart faileth me" (Psalm 40:12). King Solomon gave a stern warning about iniquities: "His own iniquities shall take the wicked himself, and he shall be holden with the cords of his sins. He shall die without instruction, and in the greatness of his folly he shall go astray" (Proverbs 5:22–23). Iniquity is not a simple or single act of sin. It is a deliberate lifestyle that is in rebellion against God and will lead into bondage to sin.

Transgression is the willful repeating of sin. To lead a life that is purposefully in opposition to the Word of God is to live in transgression. If left unchecked, the transgressions can lead to iniquities and bondage deep into sin.

A sin is a single offense against God. All unrighteousness is sin (1 John 5:17). We also know that whatsoever is not of faith is sin (Romans 14:23). James declared that omission of good work is sin: "Therefore to him that knoweth to do good, and doeth it not, to him it is sin" (James 4:17).

The holy scriptures are very clear that all have sinned: "For all have sinned, and come short of the glory of God" (Romans 3:23). None can claim to be faultless.

The order of sinfulness in God's statement to Moses is interesting to me. Perhaps God wanted to assure Moses that all sinfulness can be forgiven, and there are none so deep into sin that God's love can't reach them. To me, it seems that God was saying, "I will forgive those trapped in twisted, perverted, and terrible sin. I will forgive those who are defiantly walking away from me. And I will also forgive those who are trying to follow me but mess up and fail every day."

...And That by No Means Will Clear the Guilty

וְנַקֵּה לֹא יְנַקֶּה פֹּקֵד

We see from the Holy Bible that God created the heaven and the earth (Genesis 1:1). He chose to create humankind, and He blessed us with a beautiful world in which to live. God is worthy of His power and of our obedience because He is our creator. "Thou art worthy, O Lord, to receive glory and honour and power: for thou hast created all things, and for thy pleasure they are and were created" (Revelation 4:11). God gives humankind every good gift He enjoys. It is because of God's favor that we live and move and have our being (Acts 17:28). God is God. We are not. He is the boss. He has decided what constitutes sin and has given us explicit instructions in His Word, the Holy Bible.

There is a penalty for sin, and all sin must be punished. God's nature will not allow sin to be ignored and dismissed. The holiness of God demands reverence and obedience. God is holy, and He inhabits heaven and eternity. For us to dwell with Him, our sins must be cleansed. No sins can enter with us into heaven.

God would not be just if He allowed willful sin and disobedience to go unpunished. Though God's mercy endures and His grace is extended to every generation, sin must ultimately be judged, and the penalty for it paid. God is a just, fair, and upright judge. "But the LORD shall endure for ever: he hath prepared His throne for judgment. And he shall judge the world in righteousness, he shall minister judgment to the people in uprightness" (Psalm 9:7–8).

When God stated that He would by no means clear the guilty, He was saying, in no uncertain terms, that justice would be served. We see little justice in this present world, but justice will be served for each individual after this world. "And as it is appointed unto men once to die, but after this the judgment" (Hebrews 9:27).

God is a gentleman, so to speak. He will not force His will on any individual. We are not puppets without a choice in our eternal destinies. God allows each individual to accept the sacrifice so lovingly given or to reject the blood of His dear Son, Jesus.

It is a dangerous decision to disregard the precious blood Jesus spilled on the cross at Mount Calvary. The gospel writer John explains the condemnation:

> That whosoever believeth in him should not perish, but have eternal life. For God so loved the world, that he gave his only begotten Son, that whosoever believeth in him should not perish, but have everlasting life. For God sent not his Son into the world to condemn the world; but that the world through him might be saved. He that believeth on him is not condemned: but he that believeth not is condemned already, because he hath not believed in the name of the only begotten Son of God. (John 3:15–18)

John continues in verse 36, "He that believeth on the Son hath everlasting life: and he that believeth not shall not see life; but the wrath of God abideth on him."

The writer of Hebrews told us, "It is a fearful thing to fall into the hands of the living God" (Hebrews 10:31). God has a consistent record of judging sin. When Lucifer sinned and presumed that he would exalt himself to be like the Most High, God cast him out of heaven (Isaiah 14: 12–14). When Adam ate of the forbidden fruit, God put him out of the garden (Genesis 3:23–24). When humankind grew so wicked that every imagination and thought was only evil, God brought the great flood to judge the world (Genesis 6:5, 17). The cities of Sodom and Gomorrah were so wicked in their iniquities that God judged them with fire (Genesis 19).

Some sadly believe that God would never pass judgment because He is a God of love. He is most assuredly a God of love. But to deny His judgment is to refute history and to deny the character of God.

Jesus will be our judge (Romans 2:16; 2 Timothy 4:1). His judgments will be fair and just (John 5:30). Every individual will stand before Christ in judgment someday (Isaiah 45:23; Romans 14:11; Philippians 2:11). Those who have been washed clean from their sins by their faith in the finished work of Jesus will have eternity to spend in close fellowship with God.

Jesus explained that not everyone who calls Him Master or Lord will enter into heaven. Those who stand before Him with only their own righteousness will hear Him say, "I never knew you: depart from me, ye that work iniquity" (Matthew 7:21–23). John told us what final judgment would be passed on each person who rejects the work of Jesus:

> And I saw the dead, small and great, stand before God; and the books were opened: and another book was opened, which is the book of life: and the dead were judged out of those things which were written in the books, according to their works. And the sea gave up the dead which were in it; and death and hell delivered up the dead which were in them: and they were judged every man according to their works. And death and hell were cast into the lake of fire. This is the second death. And whosoever was not found written in the book of life was cast into the lake of fire. (Revelation 20:12–15)

12

Visiting the Iniquity of the Fathers upon the Children

After God proclaimed to Moses that He would not clear the guilty, He uttered a phrase that should make every loving parent take notice: "visiting the iniquity of the fathers upon the children, and upon the children's children, unto the third and to the fourth generation" (Exodus 34:7). This statement was not an isolated event, and God did not misspeak. The same thing is recorded three other times (Exodus 20:5; Numbers 14:18; Deuteronomy 5:9). At first glance, this seems to imply that God would punish the children for the sins of their fathers. This would certainly seem unfair and unjust from a holy God. We must examine these words to find an explanation.

There was an ancient Hebrew saying: "The fathers have eaten sour grapes, and the children's teeth are set on edge" (Ezekiel 18:2). The prophet Ezekiel reported that the Lord God refuted this saying. He went on to explain it is the soul that sins that shall answer for the sin, not the children of the sinner.

There are Old Testament and New Testament clarifications

of this statement. Each individual will give an account of him- or herself: "The fathers shall not be put to death for the children, neither shall the children be put to death for the fathers: every man shall be put to death for his own sin" (Deuteronomy 24:16). The prophet Jeremiah records, "In those days they shall say no more, The fathers have eaten a sour grape, and the children's teeth are set on edge. But every one shall die for his own iniquity: every man that eateth the sour grape, his teeth shall be set on edge" (Jeremiah 31:29–30).

Jesus addressed this issue during His earthly ministry:

> And as Jesus passed by, he saw a man which was blind from his birth. And his disciples asked him, saying, Master, who did sin, this man, or his parents, that he was born blind? Jesus answered, Neither hath this man sinned, nor his parents; but that the works of God should be made manifest in him. (John 9:1–2)

Jesus subsequently worked the work of God by healing the man's blindness.

Children will not be judged of God for the sins of their parents. But, unfortunately, children will usually be affected adversely by the sins of their parents, particularly when the parents' sin is committed to the extent of iniquity.

Poor Gideon had to grow up in a town of idol worshippers (Judges 6). Also because of idolatry, Abraham had to leave his country (Genesis 12). King Hezekiah's sins resulted in his descendants being taken captive and castrated for service in the new king's palace (2 Kings 20:16–18). King David struggled with lust and sexual sins (2 Samuel 11), and his son, Solomon, ended up with seven hundred wives, princesses, and three hundred concubines. Sadly, his idolatrous wives "turned away his heart" (1 Kings 11:3). The first man, Adam, is one of the greatest examples of generations being affected by one man's sin. Paul explained Adam's sin results to the Romans: "Wherefore, as by one man sin entered into the world, and death by sin" (Romans 5:12).

The sins of the fathers affecting the children and even the grandchildren is a sad reality we see too often in the world today. Few people confront sin or warn the sinner. Everyone demands the right to do what is right in his or her own eyes. This expression is mentioned repeatedly in the Old Testament. God often brought judgment on an entire nation when this was the predominant mind-set.

Some families struggle in poverty for generations due to the iniquities of the father of the previous generation. Multiple generations become ensnared and entangled with iniquities of alcohol and drug abuse because of the iniquities of one father. When children are reared in homes that do not acknowledge the one true God, there may be multiple generations who worship idol gods or have no reverence toward God.

It seems to me that it must be easier to pass on sinful behavior than to pass on godly behavior. We see examples of many in the Holy Bible who had great walks with God, and yet their children had weaker, more distant walks with Him. Samuel's children weren't nearly the men of God that he was. Though David was a man after God's own heart, he struggled. Then his sons struggled more than he did. It is important for each and every individual of each generation to seek God diligently. Individuals cannot allow the sins of their fathers to keep them in bondage or to restrict them from achieving what God has called them to do.

I feel this phrase was used by God as a further explanation of the phrase immediately preceding it. He was saying, "I will not clear the guilty. There are far-reaching consequences of sin. I will not take away all those natural consequences. It may affect the guilty individual's family for generations."

13

Conclusion

When God revealed Himself to Moses on Mount Sinai, He was revealing Himself in ways He hadn't before. He told Moses in Exodus, chapter six, that He had appeared to him by name, though He had only appeared to those before Moses as God Almighty (Exodus 6:2–3). He appeared to Moses as Yehovah. This deeper revelation of God was not only for the benefit of Moses, though God does reward those who diligently seek Him (Hebrews 11:6). The revelation benefited the children of Israel. And it greatly benefits Christians today.

God honored Moses's request to know Him and His ways and to reveal His glory. God spoke in a manner which could be understood by finite people. God chose, in these last days, to speak to us by His Son, Jesus (Hebrews 1:2). He speaks through His Word. John tells us:

> In the beginning was the Word, and the Word was with God, and the Word was God. The same was in the beginning with God. All things were made

by him; and without him was not any thing made that was made. In him was life; and the life was the light of men. (John 1:1–4)

God still wants us to seek Him and to know Him.

God introduced Himself to Moses by His proper name, Yehovah. Then He explained His proper position. He is the one true God, the almighty God. God revealed some of His core characteristics: He is merciful, gracious, longsuffering, and abundant in goodness and in truth. His mercy endures to all generations. He forgives even the most heinous sins of the vilest offenders. And He is just and fair in His judgment. He does not pardon the guilty but allows the natural consequences of the guilty one's sin.

God revealed His character to Moses so that Moses could model his own character after God's image. God reveals Himself to us today so that we may do the same.

In 2 Timothy 2:20 we read that, in a great house, there are vessels of honor and also vessels of dishonor. The difference between the two involved the vessels of honor receiving water and giving water for use in the house. The vessels of dishonor only receive. As Christians, we have been blessed to witness the glory of the LORD. We have the indwelling of God's Holy Spirit. We are recipients of the character of God. We must strive to allow God's character to flow from us so that we may truly conform to the image of Jesus (Romans 8:29).

Works Cited

Gregory, John Milton. *The Seven Laws of Teaching*, 1886.
Baker Publishing Group, Ada, MI.
www.hebrew4christians.com
www.philosophyofreligion.com
www.studylight.org

Printed in the United States
By Bookmasters